# The Nutrition Alphabet

## by

## Paige A. Jones, RD

This book is dedicated to my wonderful husband, Bradford, and four beautiful children, Brody, Bailey, Bianca and newborn Brooklyn

Special thanks to Brian Frederick for all his contributions into text modification and illustration ideas

**B** is for Banana
you'll always want more

# D is for Delicious
## when they're eaten with lunch

**I** is for the Importance
of a well-balanced meal

**J** is for Juice
100 percent is ideal

L is for Legumes
that have fiber as a source

These include beans,
peas and lentils of course!

**P** is for Protein
found in nuts, fish and meat

**The Food Guide Pyramid
will teach you what's okay**

**S is for Sugar, cavities galore**

**Not one, but two, or three, maybe four!**

**Once you get started
you won't want to quit**

**Z is for the Zero regrets you'll have once you try it**

**Because your health depends on it from A to Z**

# About the Author

Paige A. Jones is a registered dietitian with the American Dietetic Association. She has a Master's degree in Nutrition Science with an emphasis in Nutrition Education. She is also a certified nutrition support dietitian. Paige has always had a love and desire to educate others, especially children, about the importance of nutrition and healthy eating. Raising children of her own inspired her to create an educational tool that would introduce children to nutrition concepts in a fun and creative way.

Printed in the United States

92780LV00002BB